DEADLIEST ANIMALS

POISON DART FROG

BY GOLRIZ GOLKAR

WWW.APEXEDITIONS.COM

Copyright © 2023 by Apex Editions, Mendota Heights, MN 55120. All rights reserved. No part of this book may be reproduced or utilized in any form or by any means without written permission from the publisher.

Apex is distributed by North Star Editions:
sales@northstareditions.com | 888-417-0195

Produced for Apex by Red Line Editorial.

Photographs ©: Shutterstock Images, cover, 1, 4–5, 6, 7, 8, 10–11, 12, 13, 15, 16–17, 19, 22–23, 25, 26–27, 29; Francesco Tomasinelli/Science Source, 18–19; iStockphoto 20–21

Library of Congress Control Number: 2022901421

ISBN
978-1-63738-285-1 (hardcover)
978-1-63738-321-6 (paperback)
978-1-63738-392-6 (ebook pdf)
978-1-63738-357-5 (hosted ebook)

Printed in the United States of America
Mankato, MN
082022

NOTE TO PARENTS AND EDUCATORS
Apex books are designed to build literacy skills in striving readers. Exciting, high-interest content attracts and holds readers' attention. The text is carefully leveled to allow students to achieve success quickly. Additional features, such as bolded glossary words for difficult terms, help build comprehension.

CHAPTER 1
A COLORFUL CREATURE 4

CHAPTER 2
FROG BODIES 10

CHAPTER 3
LIFE IN THE WILD 16

CHAPTER 4
BRIGHT BUT DEADLY 22

COMPREHENSION QUESTIONS • 28
GLOSSARY • 30
TO LEARN MORE • 31
ABOUT THE AUTHOR • 31
INDEX • 32

CHAPTER 1

A COLORFUL CREATURE

A golden poison dart frog sits on a tree branch. The frog spots a beetle nearby. Its tongue darts out. The frog snatches the beetle and swallows it whole.

Golden poison dart frogs live in rain forests in Colombia.

Suddenly, the frog hears a sound. A toucan is looking for food. It swoops down to grab the frog. Then it notices the frog's bright-yellow skin.

The golden poison dart frog is one of the most poisonous animals on Earth.

Toucans eat frogs, fruit, and insects.

FAST FACT
One golden poison dart frog has enough poison to kill 10 people.

The bright color means the frog is poisonous. The toucan flies away. The frog stays safe.

DEADLY DEFENSE

Poison dart frogs don't use their poison to hunt or attack. Instead, the poison hurts anything that touches their bodies. This poison can be deadly to both humans and animals.

◀ Some poison dart frogs have spots and stripes.

CHAPTER 2

FROG BODIES

There are more than 175 types of poison dart frogs. Each has its own kind of poison. The frogs have different colors and patterns, too.

Poison dart frogs can be blue, orange, yellow, red, green, or black.

A poison dart frog's skin can help it blend in with the forest floor.

Some poison dart frogs blend in with their surroundings. Others stand out. Their colors warn **predators** to stay away.

FROG SOUNDS

Poison dart frogs make many sounds to communicate. Males have a throat pouch that fills with air. It makes deep sounds. Frogs use the sounds to ask for help and call for mates.

A frog's throat pouch gets very big when it fills with air.

Poison dart frogs use their long, sticky tongues to catch food. They eat insects. The frogs' feet are sticky, too. Their pads can cling to plants.

FAST FACT

Unlike many frogs, poison dart frogs do not have **webbed** toes.

Poison dart frogs mostly live on the ground. But they can climb trees and plants.

CHAPTER 3

LiFE iN THE WiLD

Poison dart frogs live in Central and South America. They are found in **tropical rain forests**.

Poison dart frogs live in pairs or small groups.

Tadpoles use their gills to breathe underwater.

Female frogs lay eggs in dark and wet places. Each female can lay up to 40 eggs at once. After about two weeks, **tadpoles** hatch. They have **gills** and tails.

Female poison dart frogs often lay their eggs on plant leaves near water.

FIGHTING FROGS

Poison dart frogs often fight one another. Males wrestle to get mates or homes. Females fight over places to lay their eggs.

FAST FACT
Most poison dart frogs grow to be about 1 inch (2.5 cm) long.

The parents carry the tadpoles to water. The tadpoles keep growing there. After 10 weeks, the tadpoles have legs. Their gills and tails disappear. They can live on land.

◀ **Poison dart frog parents carry their tadpoles on their backs.**

CHAPTER 4

BRIGHT BUT DEADLY

Poison dart frogs are not born poisonous. Their poison likely comes from their food. The frogs eat insects that feed on poisonous plants.

Frogs sometimes eat their dead skin. They shed their skin to keep it from hardening.

The poison enters the frogs' bodies as they eat. But it doesn't make them sick. Instead, the frogs release the poison through their skin.

HUNTING HELPERS

Some South American tribes use poison from frogs to hunt. They rub darts on the frogs' skin. The frogs' poison covers the darts. Hunters use these darts to shoot animals.

The Emberá people of Colombia use the Kokoe poison frog to make hunting darts. ▶

FAST FACT

Fire-bellied snakes can eat poison dart frogs. They don't get sick from the frogs' poison.

The poison makes the frogs taste bad. It can also hurt or kill predators. If a predator bites a frog, it will learn to stay away.

Poison dart frogs may live up to 15 years in the wild.

COMPREHENSION QUESTIONS

Write your answers on a separate piece of paper.

1. Write a few sentences describing the main ideas of Chapter 4.

2. Do you think blending in to hide from predators or using bright colors to warn them is a better defense? Why?

3. Which body part releases a poison dart frog's poison?

    A. its feet
    B. its skin
    C. its tongue

4. What could happen if a poison dart frog stopped eating insects that contained poison?

    A. The frog's body would make more poison.
    B. The frog would no longer be poisonous.
    C. The frog would attack more predators.

5. What does **cling** mean in this book?

The frogs' feet are sticky, too. Their pads can cling to plants.

- **A.** to fall off
- **B.** to run past
- **C.** to hold on tightly

6. What does **wrestle** mean in this book?

Poison dart frogs often fight one another. Males wrestle to get mates or homes.

- **A.** to grab and push
- **B.** to share space
- **C.** to share food

Answer key on page 32.

GLOSSARY

communicate
To send and receive messages.

gills
Body parts that tadpoles use to breathe underwater.

mates
Pairs of animals that come together to have babies.

predators
Animals that hunt and eat other animals.

rain forests
Areas with many trees and lots of rain.

tadpoles
Young frogs that have gills and tails and live in water.

tribes
Groups of people who share a language, customs, and beliefs.

tropical
Having weather that is often warm and wet.

webbed
Joined together with a thin layer of skin.

BOOKS

Clausen-Grace, Nicki. *Red-Eyed Tree Frogs*. Mankato, MN: Black Rabbit Books, 2019.

Grack, Rachel. *Poison Dart Frogs.* Minneapolis: Bellwether Media, 2019.

Zalewski, Aubrey. *Poison Dart Frogs*. North Mankato, MN: Capstone Press, 2020.

ONLINE RESOURCES

Visit **www.apexeditions.com** to find links and resources related to this title.

ABOUT THE AUTHOR

Golriz Golkar is a former elementary school teacher. She has written more than 50 nonfiction books for children. She loves to sing and spend time with her young daughter.

INDEX

B
blending in, 12

C
Central America, 16
colors, 6, 9, 10, 12

E
eggs, 18–19

F
feet, 14

G
golden poison dart frogs, 4, 6–7, 9

I
insects, 4, 14, 22

M
mates, 13, 19

P
patterns, 10
predators, 12, 27

R
rain forests, 16

S
skin, 6, 24
sounds, 13
South America, 16, 24

T
tadpoles, 18, 21
tongues, 4, 14

ANSWER KEY:
1. Answers will vary; 2. Answers will vary; 3. B; 4. B; 5. C; 6. A